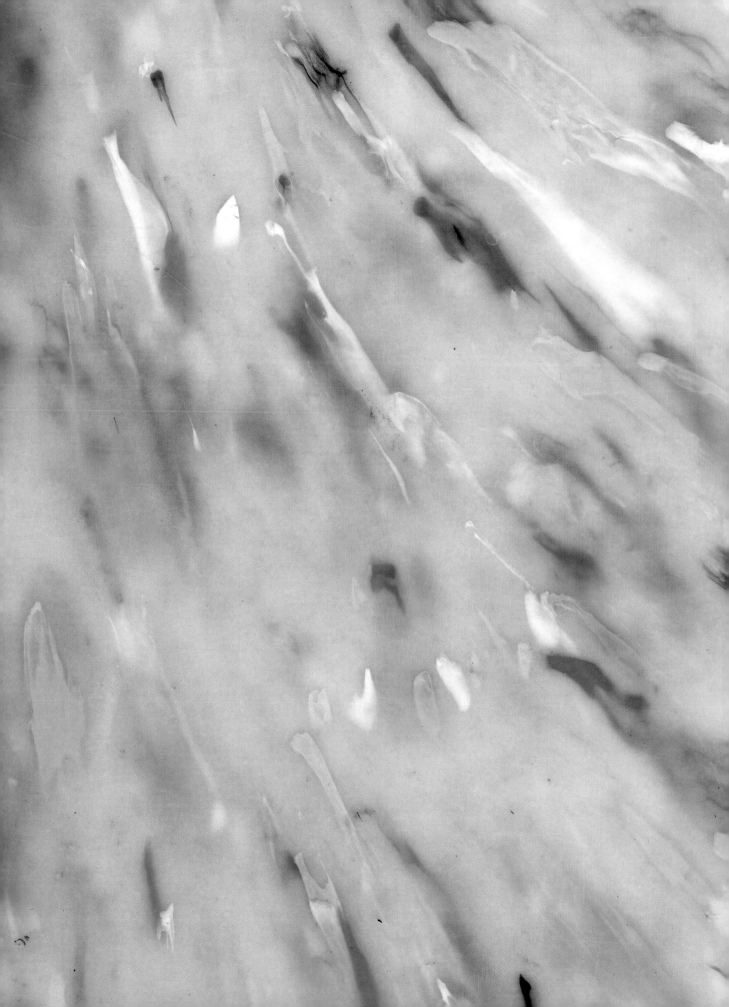

recycling & reusing

Plastics

Ruth Thomson

Photography by Neil Thomson

A+

Smart Apple Media

First published in 2006 by Franklin Watts
338 Euston Road, London NW1 3BH

Franklin Watts Australia, Hachette Children's Books
Level 17/207 Kent Street, Sydney NSW 2000

Editor: Rachel Cooke, Design: Holly Mann, Art Director: Rachel Hamdi, Consultant: Dr Mercia Gick,
British Plastics Federation

Additional photography
Franklin Watts 6cr, 6bl, 7, 8tr, 9tr, 10tr, 11cr, 13br, 19cl, 19bl, 23tl, 23cl, 24bl, 25tr, 25tl; Recycle
now 11l, 11tr, 11cl, 12l, 19tr, 22cr; Jenny Matthews 18r, 21b; Smile Plastics 26b, 27b;
Sankey Plastics 26t.

Published in the United States by Smart Apple Media
2140 Howard Drive West, North Mankato, Minnesota 56003

Library of Congress
Cataloging-in-Publication Data

Thomson, Ruth, 1949-
Plastics / by Ruth Thomson.
p. cm. — (Recycling and reusing)
Includes index.
ISBN-13: 978-1-58340-938-1
1. Plastics—Recycling—Juvenile
literature. I Title.

TP1175.R43T56 2006
668.4'192—dc22   2006000078

9 8 7 6 5 4 3 2 1

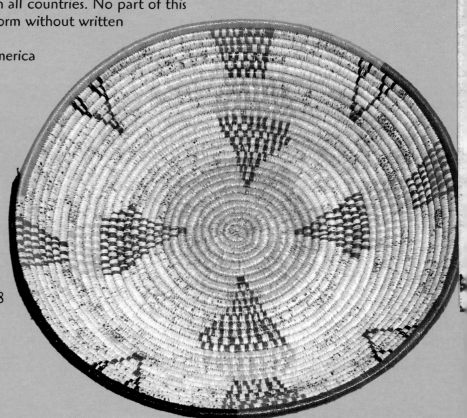

Contents

What are plastics like?

Plastics are a very useful modern **material**. They can be made into any shape, including hollow containers, long tubes, flat sheets, or thin **fibers**. Many plastics are colorful—others are white or see-through.

Some plastics are hard, stiff, and strong. They can be shaped to make sturdy things such as bowls, boxes, buckets, furniture, and storage bins.

Some plastics are soft, thin, and squishy. They can be stretched, rolled, or folded. Soft plastics are used to make bags, shower curtains, and plastic wrap.

6

Plastic is very light compared to glass or metal.
Many bottles are made of plastic. They are lighter to transport than glass ones and do not break if you drop them.

Plastics are waterproof. They do not let water in or out.

Outdoor equipment is often made of plastic because it does not **rot** like wood or **rust** like steel in wet weather.

LOOK AND SEE

How many things can you find at home or at school that are made of plastic?

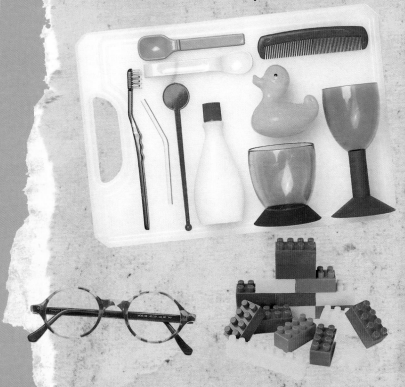

If there were no plastic, what materials could be used to make these things?

Washable

Plastic things are easy to keep clean. They do not stain or mark easily. They last a long time.

Making plastic

Some plastics are made from **natural materials**, but most are made from **chemicals** in **crude oil**. The oil is heated so that it separates. The lightest oil is used to make plastic **granules**. These are sent to **factories** that make them into products.

Melting and molding

The plastic is heated until it melts into a syrupy **liquid**. This can be shaped in a **mold**. As it cools, the plastic hardens into the shape of the mold. There are many different ways of molding plastic.

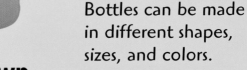

Bottles can be made in different shapes, sizes, and colors.

Squeezed

It can be squeezed through a hole to make a long tube. Hoses are made like this.

Blown

It can be blown into a mold to make a hollow object. The mold looks like the outside of the object. Bottles are made like this.

Poured

It can be poured into a mold to make solid objects, such as paperweights.

Pushed

Plastic can also be pushed under pressure through a narrow tube into a mold. This is the most common way of molding plastics. Bowls and buckets are made like this.

LOOK AND SEE

Look on the bottom of a bowl or tub. You will see a bump in the center. This is where the plastic was cut from the end of the tube.

Sheets and bags

To make plastic sheets, plastic is formed into a tube.

1. A jet of air blows the tube up like a balloon.

2. A series of rollers stretch and then flatten the plastic into thin sheets.

Saving plastic

People often throw away plastic **packaging** such as bottles, tubs, or wrapping after only one use. These fill up **landfill sites** because they do not rot easily. Some plastics can be burned as fuel to provide heat and electricity, but we need to be more careful with plastic.

Ready refills

This biker is delivering large bottles of water to offices. When the bottles are empty, he will collect them so they can be refilled.

Anyone for oil?

In Morocco, traders go from house to house refilling empty cooking oil bottles.

Assorted sweets

This shop in Egypt **reuses** clear plastic CD holders to display candy.

YOU CAN HELP

Find ways to use less plastic.

REDUCE

Persuade your family to:

- Buy refill packages instead of new bottles of detergent.

- Pick fresh fruit and vegetables rather than ones prepackaged in plastic boxes.

- Choose plastic containers that can be **recycled**. These will usually have a sign like this.

- Buy goods with as little plastic packaging as possible or in reusable containers.

REUSE

- Keep containers with lids as storage boxes.

- Wash and reuse plastic plates and cutlery.

- Plant seeds in yogurt containers, food trays, or egg boxes.

- If you take your lunch to school, put food in a lunchbox and drink in a reusable bottle.

RECYCLE

- Wash and squash plastic bottles and remove the caps. Put the bottles into a recycling bin or leave them out for recycling collection.

Reusing plastic

People have thought of clever ways to reuse plastic things instead of throwing them away.

A scarecrow

A CD on a string twists and glints in a vegetable garden to scare away any hungry birds.

A shiny lampshade

Several CDs glued together make up this lampshade. Light glows through the holes as well as from underneath.

A musical handbag

Two old records sewn onto a piece of inner tube from a truck tire make a unique handbag.

Made for sweeping

This brush and broom are made of strips cut from plastic water bottles.

Brush

Broom

A soapdish

The upturned base of a plastic bottle has been turned into a soap dish.

A perfect paint palette

Bottle caps become paint holders set into a hardboard palette.

YOUR TURN

What could you make with an old plastic bottle?

A model

You could make a model.

A rain gauge

You could cut a bottle in two and upturn the top half inside the bottom half to make a rain gauge.

Use this outside to measure how much rain falls.

Junk or treasure?

In South Africa, unemployed people were paid to clean up beaches. Most of the garbage was plastic and was sent straight to landfill sites. One group decided to earn money by making things with the waste they found.

Bright beads

People string bottle caps and pieces of plastic hoses onto old rope to make bead curtains.

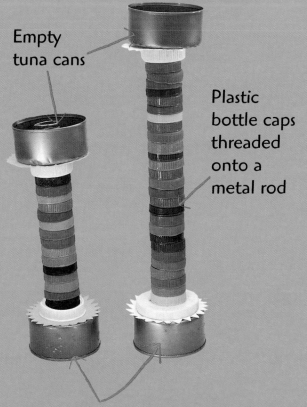

Empty tuna cans

Plastic bottle caps threaded onto a metal rod

Tuna cans filled with cement to make a solid base

Crazy candlesticks

They also make unusual candlesticks with bottle caps.

Stars cut from plastic bottles

A washing powder ball

A star attached to a bottle cap

Christmas tree decorations

The group also creates unusual Christmas tree decorations.

Junky jewelry

They make plastic jewelry, too.

Necklace made of plastic circles

Make a collection of different-colored bottle caps.

Use them as game pieces for tic-tac-toe, checkers, or other board games.

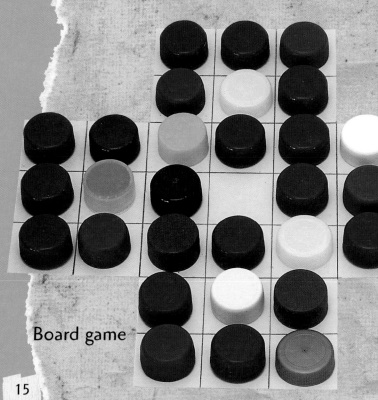

Board game

Too good to throw away

Some food and juice packets are made of layers of plastic and metal **foil**. The packaging keeps out air so that the contents stay fresh, but it is hard to recycle. Some people save it for making things.

A proud peacock

Every feather of this bird is a carefully folded food wrapper. The wings and tail are also food wrappers.

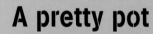

A pretty pot

More than 100 food wrappers decorate this plastic pot.

A bright bag

This bag from the Philippines is made of panels from juice packets sewn together.

Time to dress up

These children are
celebrating the Muslim
festival of Id. Their
party blowers are
covered with sparkly
food wrappers.

Cardboard
party hats
covered with
food wrappers

Party blowers made with candy wrappers

Plastic bags

In the past, people took their own bags or baskets when they went shopping. Now stores provide plastic bags. These are cheap, light, and strong, but people often throw them away carelessly.

A sign of the times

Billions of flimsy bags end up as garbage after a single shopping trip. In many places, these blow around city streets, clog drains and waterways, litter beaches, and choke animals. Many countries are now encouraging people to use fewer bags.

Bag ban

In Bangladesh, plastic bags blocked storm drains, causing flooding, so the government banned them. Now people shop with cloth bags woven from **jute**.

A bag for life

Many supermarkets sell large, strong shopping bags for people to use every time they shop. Other supermarkets offer a small refund if you bring your own bags or charge extra if you use theirs.

YOU CAN HELP

REFUSE

- Say NO to a plastic bag if you buy something small or easy to carry.

REDUCE

- Encourage your family to use a cloth bag, a basket, or a box for their shopping. Design your own logo for a cloth bag.

- Avoid putting things with handles into bags.

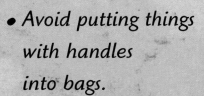

- Count how many plastic bags your family uses each week. Can you reduce the number week by week?

- Buy garbage bags made from recycled plastic.

REUSE

- Keep used plastic bags together in a handy place. Reuse them for shopping or storage.

- Give clean, unwanted plastic bags to charity shops.

Bags of ideas

Thrown-away plastic bags are a useful free raw material for craftworkers without a great deal of money.

Crochet crafts

1. This South African craftswoman cuts a plastic bag into a long, narrow, continuous strip.

2. She **crochets** the strip with a hook to create a hat, a handbag, or a basket.

These two craftswomen display some of the things that they have made from plastic bags.

Colorful chickens

Some years ago, a group of South Africans made funny chickens from discarded supermarket plastic bags and wire. They sold them on the street to passers-by and tourists.

Now people in South Africa have to pay for supermarket bags, so thrown-away ones are harder to find. Craftsmen buy cheap recycled plastic sheeting from factories. They use this to make all sorts of different animals.

What a ball!

Children in Africa cannot always afford to buy soccer balls, so they make their own. They squash old plastic bags into a ball shape and skillfully tie them tightly together with knotted plastic strips.

Recycling plastics

Almost all plastics can be recycled. Most recyclable plastics come from packaging, especially bottles and clear plastic wrap.

Recycling bottles

1. People sort bottles by type and color. Different types cannot be recycled together because they melt at different temperatures.

2. Each type is squashed and tied into a **bale** to transport to a plastics factory. At the factory, a grinder chops the bottles up into tiny **flakes**.

3. The flakes are washed, dried, and then melted. The soft plastic is pushed through a screen and comes out in long strings. After cooling, these are chopped into **pellets**, which factories buy for making new products.

LOOK AND SEE

Most plastics have long names. The names of the seven major types have been shortened and given a number. Look on plastic objects for a number. It helps people sort plastic for recycling.

4
LDPE

Light, often see-through, stretchy, easy to seal with heat

Bread, frozen vegetable, and dry cleaning bags, some plastic wrap

1
PET

Clear, hard, tough, glossy, no seams

Soft drink, water, and vegetable oil bottles, dishwashing liquid and liquid soap bottles, honey, peanut butter, and pickle jars

5
PP

Hard, smooth, cannot scratch

Screw-on caps, ketchup and medicine bottles, yogurt, ice cream, and margarine containers, woven plastic bags

2
HDPE

Strongly colored, matte (not shiny), stiff, waxy

Milk, juice, liquid detergent, shampoo, and household cleanser bottles, most shopping and garbage bags

6
PS

Light, fluffy, stiff, snaps easily

Disposable plates, tubs, and cups and lids, meat trays, egg cartons, hot drink cups

Also rigid, transparent, shiny
CD boxes and tape cases

3
PVC

Strong, smooth, resistant to oil, grease, and chemicals

Clear trays and bottles, some plastic wrap

7
OTHER

Multilayered mixed plastics

Snack bags, food wrappers

New plastic from old

Most recycled plastic is not pure enough to be used for food and drink packaging, but it can be made into many other useful household things.

Recycled carpet **underlay**

Fine fibers

Some recycled plastic is made into stuffing for ski jackets, quilts, pillows, and sleeping bags. It is also spun into thin, strong fibers used for making clothes, backpacks, and carpets.

IT'S A FACT

Some plastic starts as a syrupy liquid and sets only once. Once it is hard, it cannot become liquid again, just like boiling an egg.

Others can melt and harden again and again, just like candle wax. Only this kind of plastic can be recycled.

25 two-liter soda pop bottles were needed to make this recycled fleece.

Pots for plants

Flowerpots are often made from recycled plastic.

Brushes and brooms

Some factories dye and pull recycled plastic into long strings. They cut the strings into short bundles to make bristles for all sorts of brushes and brooms.

Bundle of bristles

Cleaning brush bristles

Scrubbing brush bristles

Broom bristles

Fantastic plastic

Recycled plastic can be found in unexpected places.

Recycled plastic rain barrel

Great for the garden

Recycled plastic is strong and does not rot. It is often used instead of wood or cement to make garden and park equipment, such as rain barrels, fencing, walkways, picnic tables, and benches. It is also used for road cones and signposts.

Cool counters

Speckled recycled plastic is very decorative. People use it to make shop counters, kitchen counters, sinks, and tubs.

A curious kennel

Can you believe it? This kennel is made from recycled toothpaste tubes. The plastic and aluminum tubes are shredded into tiny pieces, heated at a high temperature, and pressed. The plastic bits melt and stick to the aluminum bits.

Funky furniture

Designers are **experimenting** with recycled plastic as a material for furniture. The colored flecks are the colors of the original plastics, all mixed up.

Rocking lounger

Glossary

bale a large bundle

chemicals substances that are used to make materials

crochet make stitches by twisting thread or wool around a single needle

crude oil a thick black liquid found under the ground or the sea

experiment try something new

factory a building where things are made in large numbers using machines

fiber a thin thread of material

flake a small, thin, flat piece of something

foil a very thin sheet of metal

granule a small grain

jute a tall plant with strong, stringy fibers used to make bags, ropes, sacks, and carpet backs

landfill site a huge pit in the ground where crushed garbage is buried

liquid a runny substance that has no shape of its own

material a substance used to make something else

mold a block of wood, metal, or other material hollowed out into the shape of an object; melted plastic is poured into a mold to take on its shape

natural material a material made by nature, not by people

packaging the protective wrapper or container for goods

pellet a small, hard, round object formed by pressing, rolling, and cutting

recycle use an existing object or material to make something new

reuse use again

rot the natural way a material slowly breaks down into lots of smaller, different substances

rust become brown and flaky

underlay a thick padding put between a floor and a carpet

Guess what?

- About 10 percent of the weight of your household garbage is plastic.

- More than half of the litter that is found on beaches is plastic.

- Six plastic bottles weigh the same as one glass bottle of the same size.

- All plastics use up only four percent of the world's oil supply—the rest is used for transportation and electricity.

Useful Web sites

http://www.astc.org/exhibitions/rotten/rthome.htm
Learn the Rotten Truth About Garbage with interesting facts about the world's dumps and what happens to garbage

http://www.epa.gov/recyclecity/
See how Dumptown became Recycle City with fun games and interesting facts about recycling plastics and other materials

http://www.olliesworld.com/planet/
A fun, interactive site for children, that includes information and tips on recycling plastics and packaging

http://www.planetpals.com/earthday.html
Projects and information about Earth Day, America Recycles Day, and other events that promote recycling

http://www.thomasrecycling.com/kids.html
Tips, facts, and information about recycling

Index

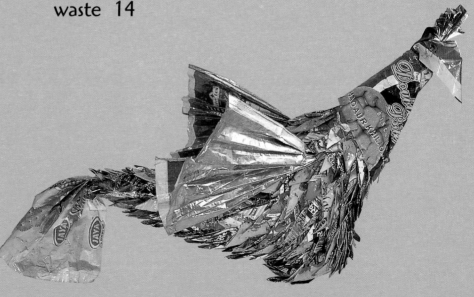

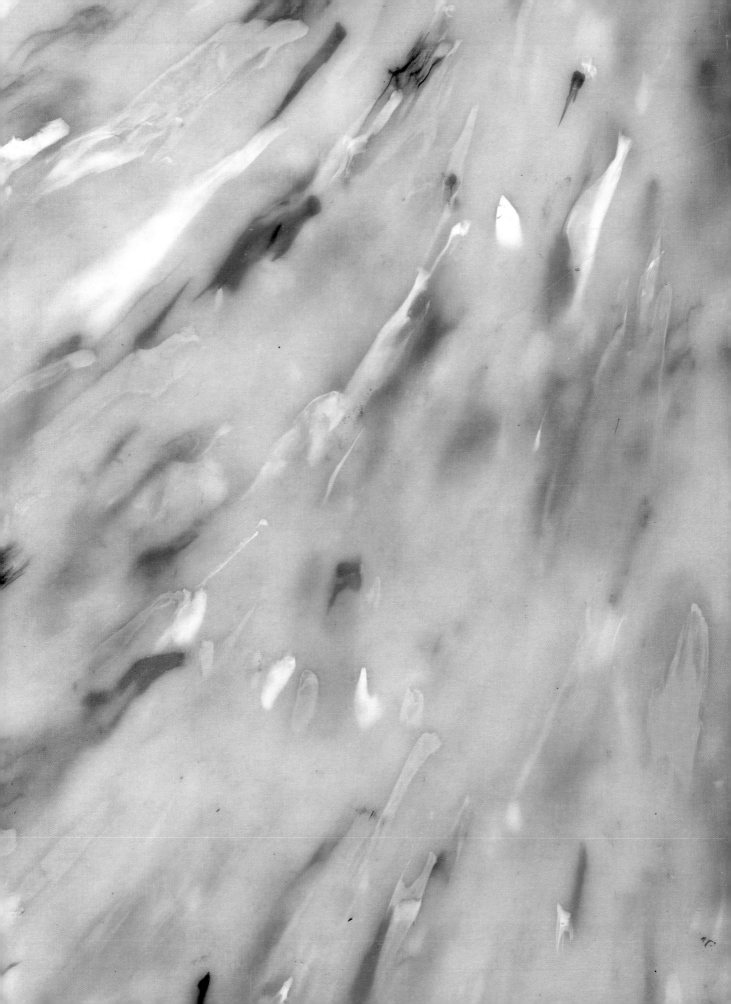